BEYONCÉ

THE VOICE THAT SHAPED A GENERATION

THE RISE OF A SUPERSTAR

Text copyright © 2025 by Patricia Pete and Ryan G. Van Cleave
Illustrations copyright © 2025 by Ariyana Taylor

All rights reserved.

Published by Bushel & Peck Books, a family-run publishing house in Fresno, California, that believes in uplifting children with the highest standards of art, music, literature, and ideas. Find beautiful books for gifted young minds at www.bushelandpeckbooks.com.

Type set in LTC Kennerley Pro, Special Elite, Nexa Rust Sans, Josefin Sans, and AltaCalifornia.

Bushel & Peck Books is dedicated to fighting illiteracy all over the world. For every book we sell, we donate one to a child in need—book for book. To nominate a school or organization to receive free books, please visit www.bushelandpeckbooks.com.

LCCN: 2025932942
ISBN: 978-1-63819-317-3

First Edition

Printed in the United States

1 3 5 7 9 10 8 6 4 2

BLACK HISTORY HEROES

BEYONCÉ

THE VOICE THAT SHAPED A GENERATION

THE RISE OF A SUPERSTAR

PATRICIA PETE WITH RYAN G. VAN CLEAVE
ILLUSTRATED BY ARIYANA TAYLOR

MILK + COOKIES

Contents

CHAPTER 1:
The Birth of a Star..................................7

CHAPTER 2:
Destiny's Child: The Girl Group
That Rocked the World............................15

CHAPTER 3:
Independent Woman: Going Solo 24

CHAPTER 4:
More Than Just Music:
The Actress and Style Icon......................33

CHAPTER 5:
Love and Family: Beyoncé and Jay-Z.........42

CHAPTER 6:
Queen Bey: Reign Over the
Music Industry 52

CHAPTER 7:
Lemonade and Legacy:
Addressing Social Issues 60

CHAPTER 8:
Reinventing the Queen:
Renaissance and Cowboy Carter...............69

CHAPTER 9:
The Business Mogul: Building
an Empire...80

CHAPTER 10:
A Legacy That Inspires 90

Glossary 97

Timeline..101

Selected Bibliography................................103

1

The Birth of a Star

I know what it's like to want to sing so badly but not have the courage to open your mouth.

—BEYONCÉ KNOWLES

Did you ever have a dream so big, you weren't sure if you were brave enough to chase it? Well, Beyoncé knows a thing or two about that! Before she became one of the biggest superstars on the planet, she was just a little girl with a dream—and a lot of nerves.

It was 1990, and the energy inside a small Houston community center was electric. The annual talent show was already ready to kick off, and all eyes were on the stage. Backstage, nine-year-old Beyoncé Giselle Knowles stood with a microphone in her trembling hand. Her heart thundered in her chest.

This was her moment. Could she find the strength to enter the spotlight?

Beyoncé peeked through the curtain, scanning the audience. There they were—Mathew and Tina Knowles, her parents and most devoted supporters, beaming up at her from the front row. They gave her a reassuring smile, and that was all she needed. Tina's words from earlier echoed in her mind: *Just be yourself, Beyoncé. You've got something special—now go out there and share it.*

With a deep breath, Beyoncé stepped onto the stage. The lights were blinding, the crowd was silent, and for a split second, fear crept in. But then, the music started, and something magical happened. Beyoncé opened her mouth, and out

poured a voice far beyond her years. The audience was **mesmerized**. As she moved across the stage, her confidence grew, and when she hit her final note, the crowd exploded into applause.

Beyoncé won first place. More importantly, she discovered the thrill of performing, a feeling that would stay with her. A true game-changing moment! It wasn't just about winning a trophy; it was about realizing that she had something incredible to share with the world.

Later that night, back at home, Beyoncé sat with her parents. The excitement had settled, but the glow of victory still lingered in the air. Mathew looked at his older daughter with pride. "You've got a gift, Beyoncé. But remember, it's going to take a lot of hard work to turn that gift into something great."

Beyoncé nodded. She was ready to put in the work. This was just the beginning of her journey, and she was determined to chase her dreams, no matter what.

Beyoncé started performing everywhere she could—school events, local gatherings, you name it. She practiced her singing and dancing for hours on end, driven by the desire to be the best. That dedication paid off when she caught the attention of talent scouts. Before long, Beyoncé became part of a group called Girl's Tyme, and the adventure really began.

Beyoncé's life now revolved around music. Mathew and Tina knew their daughter had an

incredible singing voice, and they were all in. Mathew, who had been a successful sales manager, took a leap of faith—he quit his job to help Beyoncé and Girl's Tyme navigate the music world. He believed in them so much that he wanted to be their manager, to help them make decisions and reach their full potential. And Tina, who owned a popular hair salon, made sure Beyoncé stayed grounded, reminding her to be true to herself no matter how high she soared.

But let's not sugarcoat it—Girl's Tyme didn't find success overnight. In fact, they faced serious setbacks, like losing on the TV talent show *Star Search*. Ouch! But did that stop Beyoncé? Not a chance. Instead, she accepted it for the lesson it was.

As Beyoncé's confidence grew, so did her ambitions. She wasn't just aiming to be good— she wanted to be the best. And with her parents and her younger sister, Solange, by her side, there was no stopping her. Beyoncé knew this was only the beginning of something big, and greater things were just around the corner.

So, are you ready to follow Beyoncé on her journey from that tiny stage in Houston to the world's biggest arenas? You won't want to miss a beat of this incredible story!

WORDS TO KNOW

mesmerized: completely captivated or fascinated by something

apartheid: a system of racial segregation and discrimination

THE WORLD AT THE TIME

In 1990:
- Nelson Mandela was released from prison after twenty-seven years, marking a significant moment in the fight against **apartheid** in South Africa.
- The Hubble Space Telescope was launched into space, revolutionizing our understanding of the universe.

- The pop music scene was dominated by artists like Madonna, Whitney Houston, and Michael Jackson, who were all major influences on a young Beyoncé.

WHAT DO YOU THINK?

- How do you think Beyoncé's early experiences shaped her determination to succeed?
- Why do you think her family's support was so important in her journey?

2

Destiny's Child: The Girl Group That Rocked the World

It's not about perfection. It's about purpose.

—BEYONCÉ KNOWLES

Let's take a trip back to the early '90s. Imagine a group of six young girls from Houston, Texas, full of talent, energy, and dreams of becoming stars. They called themselves Girl's Tyme, and they were ready to take on the world. The original lineup included Beyoncé, Kelly Rowland, LaTavia Roberson, Támar (Ashley) Davis, and the sisters Nikki and Nina Taylor. These girls had big ambitions and were willing to work hard to achieve them. They spent countless hours practicing their dance moves, perfecting their harmonies, and imagining their future as the Next Big Thing in music.

In 1992, they had their chance on the stage of *Star Search*, the biggest TV talent show at the time. Can you imagine the excitement? Their oversized yellow, purple, and white jackets and high-top shoes were cool.

And the dancing, singing, and even the rapping the girls did was impressive, but the song? Not so much. "The song we did was not good," Beyoncé later admitted. They made the mistake of saving their best songs for later in the show, and the audience never got to hear them.

So, Girl's Tyme lost, and an acoustic-based Detroit rock band called Skeleton Crew went on to win the $100,000 grand prize. "We cried *so* hard," Kelly said about that defeat. "We were so heartbroken! We thought it was the end of it all."

Losing on national television could have crushed Beyoncé and her fellow musicians. But here's where things changed for the better—Beyoncé's dad saw potential in the group. After their group's misstep on *Star Search*, he dedicated all of his time to managing them. Mathew knew they needed to tighten things up, so he restructured the group, trimming it down to four members: Beyoncé, Kelly, LaTavia, and a new addition, LeToya Luckett. This fresh lineup gave the group a boost of energy.

The girls performed locally around Houston, honing their skills and building their reputation. Beyoncé's mom made sure they looked the part by designing all their stage outfits. These performances helped the group refine their sound and style, and soon, they were on the radar of record labels.

After a series of almost-there group names (Somethin' Fresh, Cliché, The Dolls, and Destiny), the group settled on Destiny's Child in 1996. As Beyoncé explained, "We got the word 'destiny' out of the Bible, but we couldn't trademark the name, so we added 'child,' which is like a rebirth of destiny."

And guess what? Things started turning around.

In 1997, the group signed with Columbia Records, marking the beginning of something BIG. Their **debut** album, *Destiny's Child*, hit the shelves in 1998. The single "No, No, No" became a hit, climbing to number three on the Billboard Hot 100. The world was starting to notice these talented young women, and they were just getting started!

But, like any good story, there were twists and turns. After their next album, *The Writing's on the Wall* (1999), which included smash hits like "Bills, Bills, Bills" and "Say My Name," internal tensions began to surface. LaTavia and LeToya, feeling frustrated with how the group was being managed, decided to part ways with Destiny's Child in early 2000. It wasn't an easy decision, and it sparked quite a bit of controversy—including a lawsuit against Mathew Knowles for breach of partnership.

Enter Michelle Williams and Farrah Franklin, who replaced LaTavia and LeToya. The group pushed forward with this new lineup, but things weren't smooth sailing just yet. After just five

months, Farrah decided to leave the group, too, citing personal reasons. This left Beyoncé, Kelly, and Michelle as a trio—a lineup that would soon take the world by storm.

Despite these challenges, Destiny's Child pushed ahead at full force. In 2001, they released their next album, *Survivor*, and it lived up to its name! The album hit number one on the Bill-

board 200 chart, and songs like "Bootylicious" and "Independent Women Part I" became **anthems of empowerment**. The trio proved they were stronger than ever, winning a Grammy for their song "Survivor" and becoming one of the most successful girl groups of all time.

Through all the ups and downs, Beyoncé, Kelly, and Michelle showed the world that **resilience**, teamwork, and staying true to yourself can take you to incredible heights. Destiny's Child was more than a music group—they were a movement.

WORDS TO KNOW

debut: the very first time someone or something is presented to the public

anthem: a song identified with a particular group or cause

empowerment: confidence and control over your own life and decisions

resilience: the ability to bounce back from tough times and keep going strong

frenzy: wild excitement

THE WORLD AT THE TIME

In 1996:
- The Tickle Me Elmo doll became the must-have toy, causing a **frenzy** in stores.
- The Spice Girls burst onto the music scene with their debut single, "Wannabe," also becoming a symbol of girl power and inspiring countless kids to embrace their individuality.
- Basketball legend Michael Jordan teamed up with Bugs Bunny and the Looney Tunes filmmakers in the

live-action/animated movie *Space Jam*.

WHAT DO YOU THINK?

- How did Destiny's Child's experiences of setbacks and lineup changes shape their success?
- Why do you think their message of empowerment connected with so many people around the world?

3

Independent Woman: Going Solo

*I don't like to gamble, but if there's one thing I'm
willing to bet on, it's myself.*

—BEYONCÉ KNOWLES

What's it like to step out from the comfort
of a group and go solo? Well, Beyoncé was
about to find out.

By the early 2000s, Destiny's Child was mas-
sively successful. They were selling out arenas,

dominating the charts, and winning awards left and right. But for Beyoncé, there was a new chapter on the horizon. She'd always been the group's standout performer, but now it was time to shine even brighter—solo style!

The decision to go her own way wasn't easy. That little voice of doubt we all sometimes hear was saying, "Can you really do this on your

own?" But Beyoncé knew to trust herself. She wanted to explore her artistic vision without any limits, and she was ready for the challenge.

Her solo journey began in 2002, not with a song, but on the big screen! She made her film debut in the spy comedy *Austin Powers in Goldmember*, playing the fierce and fabulous Foxxy Cleopatra. With her signature charm and energy, Beyoncé lit up the screen and showed the world that she was more than just a singer. This leap into acting boosted her confidence and set the stage for her next big adventure.

In 2003, Beyoncé dropped her first solo album, *Dangerously in Love*. Now, the world was watching. Could she make it in music without her Destiny's Child crew? The pressure was on, but Beyoncé was more than ready. She poured her heart and soul into the album, and it showed. The lead single, "Crazy in Love," featuring rapper Jay-Z, burst onto the scene. The song's **infectious** beat and energetic lyrics had everyone dancing, and it quickly rocketed up the charts.

But *Dangerously in Love* wasn't a one-hit wonder. The album was a musical masterpiece that showcased Beyoncé's **versatility**. From the smooth vibes of "Baby Boy" to the empowering "Me, Myself and I," she proved that she could dominate multiple **genres**. The world was hooked, and Beyoncé walked away with not one, not two, but FIVE Grammy Awards, including Best Contemporary R&B Album. Talk about a solo career debut!

Even with all the **accolades**, Beyoncé stayed grounded. She knew success didn't come easy. "I've paid my dues a hundred times over," she said. "I have worked harder than anyone I know." But that's what it takes—you have to earn your success every single day.

And wow, did she earn it.

Her commitment to excellence was undeniable. On her *Dangerously in Love* promotional tour, Beyoncé held nothing back, dazzling the crowd with her energy and talent. Whether she was performing in front of a sold-out arena or on a late-night talk show, she gave 110 percent. Her stage presence was electrifying, and fans couldn't get enough.

One performance in particular stood out—the 2003 BET Awards. Beyoncé opened the show in a purple and green outfit and sky-high green heels, ready to rock the house with "Crazy in Love." The moment she appeared, giant LED lights spelled out her name, and the crowd went wild. She danced, strutted, and spun across the stage like a seasoned pro. Her confidence was unmistakable, announcing she was here to stay!

Backstage, after the performance, Beyoncé's family was there to celebrate. Her mom, who

was still designing her stage clothes, hugged her tightly. "You were incredible," Tina said, beaming with pride.

Still catching her breath and coming back down to earth from such a spectacular performance, Beyoncé already knew that her family and fans hadn't seen anything yet.

And she didn't stick with just music! With her solo career in full swing, Beyoncé continued her acting career, taking on a role in the musical comedy *The Fighting Temptations*. She wasn't just dipping her toes into the acting world— she was diving in headfirst, proving again and again that her talents extended far beyond the recording studio. Whether belting out a **ballad** or delivering a powerful scene, Beyoncé showed that she could do it all. As an entertainer, she was a force of nature!

By the mid-2000s, Beyoncé had firmly established herself as one of the most successful and influential artists of her generation. From girl group member to solo superstar, her journey was a **testament** to her talent, determination, and unwavering belief in herself. But even with all her success, Beyoncé remained humble and grounded, never forgetting the values her parents had instilled in her.

"I'm so blessed to wake up every morning and do what I love," she once said. "But I know that with success comes responsibility. I want to use my platform to inspire others and make a difference in the world." And that's exactly what she did—and continues to do.

So, are you ready to see what comes next for Queen Bey? Because this is only the beginning of her solo adventure, and there's still way more to come!

WORDS TO KNOW

infectious: easily spread from one person to another

versatility: the ability to adapt to different activities or roles

genre: a category or type of art, music, or literature, characterized by its style, form, or content

accolade: an award or special recognition for achievement

ballad: a slow, emotional song that tells a story

testament: proof or evidence that something is true

THE WORLD AT THE TIME

In 2003:
- The Iraq War began. This conflict would shape global politics for years to come.
- Pixar released *Finding Nemo*, a box office hit that went on to win the

Academy Award for Best Animated Feature.
- Apple changed the music industry forever by launching the iTunes Store, making it easier than ever to purchase and listen to music.

WHAT DO YOU THINK?

- How did Beyoncé's early experiences with Destiny's Child prepare her for solo success?
- Why do you think *Dangerously in Love* was popular with so many people around the world?

4

More Than Just Music: The Actress and Style Icon

My style offstage is so different from onstage. I love a pair of sexy heels with jeans, a nice jacket, or a little dress.

—BEYONCÉ KNOWLES

Beyoncé has never been one to stay in the slow lane. From the moment she burst onto the scene, it was undeniable that her talents would take her far beyond just the music industry. With a voice that could move mountains and a stage presence that's second to none, Beyoncé has always had that megastar quality. So, it's no surprise that Hollywood kept calling.

In 2006, Beyoncé made a splash on the big screen with her role in *Dreamgirls*. Imagine this: She's playing Deena Jones, a character reportedly inspired by Diana Ross, who, like Beyoncé herself, had been the lead singer of a celebrated musical trio before beginning a legendary career as a solo artist.

The movie, based on a 1981 Broadway musical, tells the story of a **Motown** girl group's rise to fame, and Beyoncé absolutely nailed it. Her performance was so good, she even snagged a Golden Globe nomination. Not bad for someone who's known for belting out hits, right?

But here's the thing. *Dreamgirls* was more than just another acting gig for Beyoncé. It was personal. When she sang "Listen" in the movie, it was like Beyoncé was telling the world, "I'm here, and I've got something to say." The song is all about finding your voice and breaking free, and Beyoncé felt that deep in her soul.

And just like that, Beyoncé wasn't a mere singer anymore—she was a **bona fide** movie star. But she wasn't stopping there! Next up? More movies! In 2006, she starred in *The Pink Panther*, and in 2008, she took on the role of blues legend Etta James in *Cadillac Records*. When she sang "At Last" as Etta, it was pure magic. Critics couldn't stop raving about how she captured Etta's emotional depth while still bringing her signature Beyoncé flair to the role.

But Beyoncé did more than shine on the silver screen. She took the fashion world by storm too. With her mom by her side, she launched her very own clothing line, House of Deréon, in 2006. The name? It's a tribute to her grandmother Agnèz Deréon—a nod to the strong women who came before her. House of Deréon was all about blending high fashion with street style, reflecting Beyoncé's fierce and fabulous **aesthetic**.

Beyoncé has explained that fashion is an extension of who she is, and that it's not about what you wear but how you feel in it, and how you express yourself. And express herself she did! Whether she was rocking a showstopping gown on the red carpet or dazzling fans with her stage outfits, Beyoncé always turned heads and set trends. Everyone wanted to know: What's she going to wear next?

Beyoncé decided to shake things up creatively with her 2013 album, *Beyoncé*. It was a complete surprise, recorded in complete secrecy for over a year and a half. She spent much of each day with her newborn daughter, Blue Ivy, and worked most evenings with some of the world's top producers and songwriters. The result was a visual album, where each track had its own gorgeous music video that showcased Beyoncé's next-level looks and fashion. As she later said in a documentary, having videos for every song gave people the rare chance to "actually be able to see the whole vision of the album."

Beyoncé had plenty of unforgettable fashion moments that weren't tied to an album or a performance. The 2014 Met Gala, for example! Beyoncé made her entrance in a sheer black bejeweled **Givenchy** gown that instantly became the talk of the night. Some loved it, some weren't sure what to think—but one thing was for sure: Beyoncé knew how to make a statement. "My biggest thing is to teach not to focus on the aesthetic," she said. "It's really about who you are, and the human being, that makes you beautiful." And that's why she's a style **icon**—she's fearless and proud.

But here's the best part—for Beyoncé, fashion was about feeling good as much as it was about looking good. She used her style to express her confidence and independence, sending a message to women everywhere that they could be dazzling, strong, and unapologetically themselves. The outfits she wore had a deeper meaning, reflecting the powerful themes in her music and the statements she wanted to make.

As Beyoncé continued to push boundaries in both music and fashion, she proved that she was more than just a trendsetter—she was a trailblazer. She knew how to use visuals to tell a story, and every outfit, every look, was a part of that story. Whether she was performing, acting, or designing, Beyoncé blended fashion, music, and film in a way that no one else could.

But it wasn't just about blazing trails. Beyoncé

had her eyes on a bigger prize: creating a legacy. She used her platform to uplift and inspire others, especially women of color. She challenged the industry's narrow standards of beauty and representation, opening doors for more diversity and inclusion in both fashion and entertainment.

Beyoncé has never been afraid to take risks. In her mind, it's how you grow, and how you become who you were meant to be. With that mindset, she became an inspirational triple threat through her acting, her fashion, and her music.

WORDS TO KNOW

icon: a person or thing admired and recognized as a symbol of something

Motown: a legendary record label from Detroit that became the heart of soul and R&B music

bona fide: genuine, authentic, or real

aesthetic: a particular approach or style to art and beauty

Givenchy: a famous French luxury fashion and perfume house

THE WORLD AT THE TIME

In 2006:
- The PlayStation 3 arrived on the

scene, boasting powerful graphics and exciting new gaming experiences.
- Pluto was reclassified as a "dwarf planet," sparking debate among astronomers and the public.
- The world saw the introduction of the Nintendo Wii, which changed the landscape of video gaming with its motion-sensing technology.

WHAT DO YOU THINK?

- How did Beyoncé's roles in movies allow her to express different sides of her talent?
- What impact do you think Beyoncé's fashion choices have had on her career and public image?

5

Love and Family: Beyoncé and Jay-Z

Life is more meaningful when you're constantly growing and becoming a better person.

—BEYONCÉ KNOWLES

Imagine being part of one of the most famous couples in the world, where your love story is both tabloid gossip and a powerful partnership

that's changed the music industry forever. That's the life of Beyoncé and Jay-Z—a duo that's equal parts romance and business, with a whole lot of creativity in between!

Let's rewind to the early 2000s. Beyoncé was already a superstar with Destiny's Child, but something big was happening behind the scenes. She was falling in love with rapper and music **mogul** Jay-Z. But shhh—they kept it under wraps. While fans speculated, Bey and Jay were focused on building something real, away from the flashing cameras.

The world got its first hint of their chemistry in 2002 with the hit single "'03 Bonnie & Clyde." With lyrics about loyalty and love, the song and its accompanying music video left fans buzzing. Was there more to this collaboration? And then came "Crazy in Love" in 2003, and wow, did sparks fly! The track was a massive hit, and it became clear to everyone. Beyoncé and Jay-Z were making magic together beyond the music.

But here's the thing about these two: They value their privacy. Even as their star power grew, Beyoncé and Jay-Z kept their relationship out of the spotlight. "There's definitely a dangerous feeling when you're in love," Beyoncé admitted. "It's giving your heart to someone else and knowing that they have control over your feelings." And so, while the world speculated, the couple focused on what mattered most—each other.

Fast-forward to 2008. Beyoncé and Jay-Z married in a super-secret ceremony at Jay-Z's New York City penthouse. It wasn't the over-the-top affair you might expect from two of the biggest stars in the world. Instead, it was intimate and private, with only close friends and family in attendance. Beyoncé's mom designed her wedding dress, a beautiful strapless creation that was both elegant and understated.

As their love grew, so did their family. In 2012, they welcomed their first child, Blue Ivy

Carter, into the world. Blue Ivy didn't just make headlines as the daughter of music royalty—she quickly started making her own mark. Whether she was stealing the show in her mom's music videos or becoming the youngest person to win a BET Award, Blue Ivy was already showing signs of following in her parents' legendary footsteps.

Beyoncé said that marriage is a journey, a partnership, and a commitment to grow together. And grow together they did! Over the years, Beyoncé and Jay-Z collaborated on some of the most memorable music of the twenty-first century, blending their talents to create tracks that are more than just songs—they're anthems.

One of their standout collaborations happened back in 2013 with the album *Beyoncé*. Songs like "Drunk in Love" showcased their undeniable chemistry, with romantic visuals that left no doubt. These two were head over heels for each other.

But, like any relationship, theirs had its ups and downs. In 2014, a viral video showed Solange in an elevator with Jay-Z, standing up for her sister during what seemed like a heated moment. This **infamous** video led to rumors that Jay-Z hadn't been faithful, and the media couldn't stop talking about it. Instead of focusing on the drama, Beyoncé turned to what she does best. She focused on her art.

In 2016, she released *Lemonade*, a visual album that captured people's hearts with its honesty and emotion. The songs explored feelings of hurt and betrayal, but they also celebrated the power of love and forgiveness. Tracks like "Hold Up" and "Sorry" expressed deep emotions, while "All Night" showed the beauty of healing and hope. *Lemonade* became a cultural phenomenon, cementing Beyoncé as a voice for women, particularly Black women, and a force to be reckoned with. It wasn't just about her marriage—it was about finding strength in vulnerability, embracing every part of who she was, and making bold statements about race and gender along the way.

Jay-Z also addressed their struggles in his 2017 album, 4:44. In it, he apologized and reflected on his mistakes, sharing how he wanted to improve as a husband and partner. It was a moment of honesty that gave the world a glimpse into the couple's efforts to work through difficult times together.

Later that same year, Beyoncé and Jay-Z welcomed twins, Rumi and Sir, into their family. With three kids to love and care for, they focused even more on family while continuing to create amazing music together. In 2018, they released *Everything Is Love* as The Carters, celebrating their journey as a couple and as a family. One of their music videos, filmed at the **Louvre** in Paris, turned the famous museum into a backdrop for their story.

Beyoncé has shown again and again that she faces life's tests with poise and determination. Through every high and low, she has stayed true

to herself and continued to grow as a person and as an artist. Whatever the future holds, Beyoncé's story reminds us that she will always rise to meet life's challenges with confidence and grace, inspiring others along the way.

WORDS TO KNOW

mogul: a powerful and influential person in business or industry

infamous: well-known for something bad or negative

Louvre: a world-renowned art museum located in Paris, France, and home to important works like the *Mona Lisa*

THE WORLD AT THE TIME

In 2008:

- Barack Obama was elected the first Black president of the United States, inspiring hope and change worldwide.

- The first Marvel Cinematic Universe movie, *Iron Man,* was released, kicking off a superhero movie phenomenon.
- Michael Phelps made history at the Beijing Olympics, winning an incredible eight gold medals in swimming.

WHAT DO YOU THINK?

- If you could ask Beyoncé and Jay-Z one question about their love story, what would it be?
- What's your favorite song by Beyoncé or Jay-Z, and why do you like it so much?

6

Queen Bey: Reign Over the Music Industry

*I'm always thinking about women who inspire me.
I'm still so inspired by Tina Turner. I think she's
the ultimate performer. When I was a kid,
I aspired to be like her.*

—BEYONCÉ KNOWLES

Ever wonder what it takes to rise from being a solo artist to become the undisputed Queen of the music industry? Well, Beyoncé did just that. With every chart-topping album, she reshaped what it means to be a global superstar. Buckle up, because this is the story of how Beyoncé took her crown and turned it into a symbol of musical power, creativity, and excellence.

By 2006, Beyoncé was already a household name, but she wasn't done yet—not even close! That year, she celebrated her twenty-fifth birthday in style by releasing her second solo album, *B'Day*. This album gave us hits like "Déjà Vu," "Irreplaceable," and "Beautiful Liar," which became an anthem for self-worth and independence. This message struck a chord with fans worldwide.

And if you've ever seen Beyoncé perform live, you know she creates unforgettable experiences. At the 2006 BET Awards, she performed "Déjà Vu" with such energy and precision that it became a defining moment in her career. As pyrotechnics exploded behind her, she owned the stage in a metallic miniskirt and bejeweled body art. With her electrifying **choreography** and powerful vocals, it was clear to everyone watching that she was a performer in a league of her own.

Then, in 2008, Beyoncé introduced us to a new side of herself with the release of *I Am . . . Sasha Fierce*. This album showcased two sides of her personality: the **introspective** and emotional side, with songs like "If I Were a Boy," and her fearless **persona** Sasha Fierce, with hits like "Single Ladies (Put a Ring on It)." And let's talk about that "Single Ladies (Put a Ring on It)" music video—**minimalist**, black and white, and featuring an iconic dance routine that became a global sensation. Everyone, from celebrities to your next-door neighbors, was trying to master that dance.

Beyoncé explained that Sasha Fierce was a way for her to embrace her confidence and assertiveness onstage. Whether she was singing a powerful ballad or commanding the spotlight with a high-energy anthem, Beyoncé showed the world that she could do it all and look amazing while doing it.

Her *I Am . . .* World Tour was a massive success, **grossing** over $100 million. Night after night, in sold-out arenas, she switched effortlessly between the emotional depth of *I Am . . .* and the whirlwind energy of Sasha Fierce. It was a testament to her versatility and artistry, and it solidified her status as a worldwide superstar.

One of the biggest moments in her career came in 2013, when Beyoncé headlined the halftime show for Super Bowl XLVII. In a lace-and-leather bodysuit, she captivated the crowd with her high-energy dancing and awesome singing. Now, while she'd been a solo artist for a decade, she did a cool thing—she had former Destiny's Child members Kelly Rowland and Michelle Williams join her onstage to perform "Bootylicious," "Independent Women Part I," and "Single Ladies (Put a Ring on It)." They were backed by an all-female band, a thirty-two–cheerleader troupe, and an all-female horn section. That was an **innovative** idea in full alignment with Beyoncé's commitment to girl power.

The show ended with Beyoncé delivering an especially emotional rendition of "Halo." Since it was the second most-watched halftime show in history with 110 million viewers, she understood

the rare opportunity this event afforded her. So, she ended with a genuine: "Thank you for this moment. God bless y'all."

WORDS TO KNOW

choreography: the art of creating and arranging dance movements

introspective: looking inward to examine your own thoughts and feelings

minimalist: characterized by extreme simplicity of form or design

persona: a social role or character adopted by an individual

grossing: earning a certain amount of money before expenses are taken out

innovative: introducing new ideas or methods; original and creative in thinking

THE WORLD AT THE TIME

In 2013:

- *Frozen* was released by Disney, becoming one of the highest-grossing animated films of all time.

- "Selfie" was added to the *Oxford English Dictionary.*
- The Boston Marathon bombing shocked the world and led to increased security measures at public events.

WHAT DO YOU THINK?

- How did Beyoncé's creation of Sasha Fierce allow her to express different aspects of her personality?
- What do you think makes a song become an anthem for many people?

7

Lemonade and Legacy: Addressing Social Issues

The more you mature, you realize that these imperfections make you more beautiful.

—BEYONCÉ KNOWLES

When life gives you lemons, you make lemonade, right? Well, if you're Beyoncé, you take that lemonade and create something that leaves the world in awe. Her 2016 album, *Lemonade*, was a blend of art, personal reflection, and social commentary that got everyone talking. The title came from a simple moment—Jay-Z's grandmother said, "I was served lemons, but I made lemonade" at her ninetieth birthday party. As she'd done before, Beyoncé took that idea and then used her music to shake things up and make a statement.

Imagine waking up one day, grabbing your phone, and seeing a surprise album from Beyoncé. With no teasers, no announcements, *Lemonade* just dropped right into the world. Who does something like that? Beyoncé does! She did it with *Beyoncé* in 2013, and here she was, doing it again, only with a sixty-five-minute film instead of individual music videos for each song!

Lemonade hit hard. Of course it had unforgettable beats, but it also had depth and meaning. With this new album, Beyoncé took us on a journey through her personal struggles, her cultural identity, and African American history, all wrapped up in striking imagery that couldn't be ignored. She opened up about some deeply personal stuff, but it was so much more than

that. This album spoke to the experiences of Black women everywhere. From the raw emotion in "Hold Up" to the unapologetic strength in "Sorry," Beyoncé was speaking her truth.

And then there was "Formation," one of the biggest hits on *Lemonade*. When Beyoncé made her second Super Bowl halftime show appearance, this time in 2016, she made a wow-worthy statement. With dancers dressed in *Black Panther*-inspired costumes and lyrics touching on police brutality and Black pride, Beyoncé used her platform to address the issues that mattered most. The performance was bold, powerful, and completely unforgettable.

Beyond the music and the message, *Lemonade* was a visual masterpiece. The film that accompanied the music took viewers on a rich journey of African American culture and history. From women dressed in traditional African garments to the amazing **Southern Gothic** aesthetics, every frame was packed with **symbolism**. And the lines of **Warsan Shire**'s poetry that were included throughout the album? That added an extra layer of depth that made *Lemonade* a cultural treasure.

Perhaps most important, *Lemonade* was as much about healing as it was about highlighting struggles. In "Sandcastles," Beyoncé's vulnerability shone through as she sang about forgiveness and **reconciliation**. By the time we reach the second-to-last track, "All Night," we're left with a message of love triumphing over pain. It's like Beyoncé was telling us that even in the darkest times, there's always room for hope.

Released exclusively on Tidal, a streaming service owned at the time by Jay-Z, the album was a commercial phenomenon. It topped the charts, racked up awards, and proved that Beyoncé was still a force to be reckoned with in both music and culture. She'd rewritten the rules once more.

Critics and fans couldn't stop praising *Lemonade* for its innovation and emotional depth. The album sparked crucial conversations about

race, gender, and relationships, becoming a cultural milestone. And at the heart of it all was Beyoncé—fearless, honest, and ready to use her voice to inspire change.

Beyoncé once said, "It's about the journey. It's about finding your strength, finding your own power, and using your voice." And with *Lemonade*, she did just that. She turned her personal experiences into a story that **resonated** with millions.

So, next time life hands you a challenge, think of how Beyoncé turned her struggles into *Lemonade*. It's not just about surviving—it's about thriving and inspiring others to do the same. Who knows? Your own version of *Lemonade* might just change the world.

WORDS TO KNOW

Southern Gothic: a literary genre characterized by its setting in the southern United States and its focus on themes of decay, the grotesque, and social issues

symbolism: the use of objects or images to represent deeper ideas

Warsan Shire: a Somali-British poet

known for her powerful verses on themes of identity, displacement, and love

reconciliation: the act of restoring friendly relations

resonate: create a feeling of shared experience or understanding

THE WORLD AT THE TIME

In 2016:

- The app TikTok (originally called Musical.ly) was launched, paving the way for a new generation of short-form video creators.
- The musical *Hamilton*, which tells the story of American Founding Father Alexander Hamilton through hip-hop and R&B music, won the Tony Award for Best Musical.

- The Chicago Cubs won the World Series for the first time in 108 years.

WHAT DO YOU THINK?

- How did *Lemonade* change the public's perception of Beyoncé as an artist and activist?
- What role do you think artists should play in addressing social and political issues?

8

Reinventing the Queen: Renaissance and Cowboy Carter

I'm a perfectionist. I'm not going to sit back and say, "Oh, people like this, so let me do this next." I'd rather push myself to continue to improve.

—BEYONCÉ KNOWLES

Just when you think Beyoncé's reached the top, she flips the script to be bolder, fiercer, and more groundbreaking than ever. We've watched her rise from a young girl with a dream to a global superstar, but Queen Bey isn't about to slow down. If anything, she's just finding and reinventing her groove.

Enter *Renaissance* (2022) and *Cowboy Carter* (2024)—two albums that prove Beyoncé is in a league of her own, constantly pushing boundaries and redefining what it means to be an artist in the twenty-first century.

First up, *Renaissance.* Think you know Beyoncé's sound? Think again. This album is like nothing she'd done before. It's a high-energy celebration of life that draws deep from the well of Black queer culture and the pulsing beats of house music. From the moment you hit "play," *Renaissance* grabs you and doesn't let go. It's an invitation to dance, to celebrate, and to embrace who you are, no matter what the world says.

Tracks like "Break My Soul" and "Alien Superstar" are anthems for a new era where resilience and self-love reign supreme. Here, Beyoncé created a space where everyone, especially those who've been pushed to the margins, can feel seen, heard, and celebrated. *Renaissance* makes a strong statement: THIS IS OUR TIME, and we're making the most of it.

But *Renaissance* isn't just about cranking out hits. It's Beyoncé's love letter to a community that has been driving culture and creativity all along. She's taking the beats and stories of Black queer culture and making sure they get the spotlight they deserve, turning every dance floor

into a place where you can own your truth. Beyoncé's here to show us that finding joy is a powerful way to push back and stand tall.

In 2023, Beyoncé sent fans into a frenzy with the announcement of her fifty-six-show Renaissance World Tour. Blending the vibrant energy of her *Renaissance* album with stunning visuals and choreography, these concerts lasted almost three hours and featured all the songs from the new album in order, with some of Beyoncé's hits mixed in. The stage was equally unforgettable, with giant sculptures, metallic tanks, robotic arms, and both pyrotechnic and ultraviolet technology effects.

Tickets sold out in record time, proving once again that her influence is unstoppable. Even when Beyoncé got bronchitis and ongoing nasal infections from the smoke effects, she kept touring. Say it again: She. Is. Unstoppable.

Just when it seemed Beyoncé couldn't top the success of that album—the first in a planned trilogy—the second came out in 2024. "I think people are going to be surprised because I don't think this music is what everyone expects," Beyoncé said about *Cowboy Carter*, "but it's the best music I've ever made."

Cowboy Carter turned the music world on its head yet again. Country music and Beyoncé might sound like a wild combo, but Beyoncé's never been one to follow the crowd. And remember—she grew up in Texas, so she knows firsthand about cowboy culture, as well as country, gospel, and **zydeco** music.

Songs like "My Rose" and "Desert Eagle" take us on a journey through love, loss, and everything in between, with lyrics that cut deep and melodies that linger long after the music stops. But Beyoncé didn't just stick to the classic country themes. Not a chance! She used the genre to explore what it means to carve out a space for yourself in a world that often tries to put labels on you.

With *Cowboy Carter*, Beyoncé's making history. As the first Black woman to top the

Billboard Country Albums chart with the song "Texas Hold 'Em," she's breaking barriers and proving that country music is for everyone. And naturally, Beyoncé's got her signature flair all over the album, turning every note into a moment and every performance into an event. It's pure Queen Bey.

However, it's not just about the music videos, though they're spectacular as always. With sweeping landscapes and high-fashion looks, *Cowboy Carter* is a visual journey that's as rich and layered as the music itself. Beyoncé's blending the rustic charm of the American South with her own unique style, while bringing in influences from all around the world. The result is an album that critics loved and described as "genre-busting," "genre-defying," and "genre-bending."

"This ain't a country album," Beyoncé finally explained. "This is a 'Beyoncé' album."

The world agreed. At the 2025 Grammy Awards, Beyoncé won Album of the Year for *Cowboy Carter*, becoming the fourth Black woman and the first with a country album to receive the honor. She also won Best Country Album and Best Country Duo/Group Performance for "II Most Wanted" with Miley Cyrus.

These wins secured her legacy as the most-awarded artist in Grammy history, bringing her total to 35 trophies. But for Beyoncé, the moment was about something bigger. "I think sometimes genre is a code word to keep us in our place as artists," she said. "I just want to encourage people to do what they're passionate about and to stay persistent." She dedicated her win to country music trailblazer Linda Martell and reminded the world that breaking barriers takes courage.

Despite early skepticism from some in the country music industry, Beyoncé's vision for *Cowboy Carter* resonated with audiences across genres. Even country legends took notice—including one of the biggest icons of all, Dolly Parton. Dolly, who wrote "Jolene," one of the songs on *Cowboy Carter*, praised Beyoncé's work. She said, "The song has been recorded worldwide over 400 times in lots of different languages, by lots of different bands," but she'd been hoping someone would rerecord it in a powerhouse new way. Enter Beyoncé, who surpassed that goal.

What's crystal clear from both *Renaissance* and *Cowboy Carter* is that Beyoncé is constantly evolving. Whether she's celebrating the exciting energy of Black queer culture or bringing a fresh perspective to country music, Beyoncé is always ahead of the curve, always setting the standard for what's next.

And yet, through all this reinvention, there's one thing that remains constant: Beyoncé's unwavering commitment to her craft. She never chases trends—she sets them, raising the bar higher with every project she takes on.

There's no ceiling she can't smash.

So, what's next for Queen Bey? If there's one thing we know, it's that whatever she's cooking up, it'll be groundbreaking, fearless, and something we'll be talking about—and dancing to—for years.

WORDS TO KNOW

zydeco: a lively music and dance style from Louisiana that blends African

American and Creole traditions with a touch of French flair

geopolitical: relating to the influence of geography and politics on international relations

moderation: doing or having something in a balanced way

sportswashing: using sports to make people forget about bad actions or policies

THE WORLD AT THE TIME

In 2022:
- Russia launched a full-scale invasion of Ukraine, causing a devastating humanitarian crisis and **geopolitical** tensions.
- Elon Musk bought Twitter for $44 billion, leading to significant

changes to the platform and sparking debates about free speech and content **moderation.**
- The FIFA World Cup was held in Qatar, marking the first time the tournament was hosted in the Middle East and sparking discussions about human rights and **sportswashing.**

WHAT DO YOU THINK?

- Beyoncé created *Cowboy Carter* in response to feeling unwelcome in the world of country music. Think of a time when you felt like you didn't belong. What types of songs would you write about that experience?
- What do you think Beyoncé's next album might sound like?

9

The Business Mogul: Building an Empire

As soon as I accomplish one thing, I just set a higher goal. That's how I've gotten to where I am.

—BEYONCÉ KNOWLES

Picture Beyoncé onstage, lights flashing, the crowd roaring as she hits every note with precision. Now, imagine her in a boardroom, making power moves that shape industries.

While we've been captivated by her incredible performances, Beyoncé has quietly built a business empire that's as dynamic and influential as her music career. From fashion to **philanthropy**, she's become a global dynamo. Ready to dive in to how she did it?

It all started back in 2008, when Beyoncé made a bold move by creating Parkwood Entertainment, her very own entertainment and management company. This wasn't just a smart business decision—it was a declaration of independence. With Parkwood, Beyoncé took full control of her creative journey.

Whether it was producing her later groundbreaking music like *Lemonade* or visual projects like *Black Is King*—the 2020 musical film that reimagined *The Lion King* story, which she cowrote, executive-produced, and directed—Parkwood is where Beyoncé's vision comes to life. And here's the best part: She's doing it all on her own terms.

In 2010, Beyoncé expanded her empire into the world of beauty with the launch of Heat, her first signature fragrance. Like everything she touches, it turned to gold, quickly becoming one of the best-selling celebrity fragrances of all time. With follow-up scents like Pulse and Rise, Beyoncé continued to find success in the beauty industry.

Next up was fashion. In 2016, Beyoncé launched her **athleisure** line, Ivy Park, initially in partnership with Topshop, a British **fast fashion** women's clothing company. By 2018, she'd taken full control of the brand, and in 2019, she teamed up with Adidas to take Ivy Park to new heights. The company's mission? "To be the best sports brand in the world." Of course, that's a Beyoncé-level goal.

Here's the real magic of Ivy Park: Beyoncé made sure her brand was inclusive, with sizes and styles that embrace diversity. In a world that often tries to tell us what we should look like, Ivy Park rewrites the rules. A few years later, she turned heads again with her Icy Park collection, a winter-ready twist that had everyone talking—and, of course, it sold out in no time.

But Beyoncé's empire isn't just about making waves in fashion and beauty. It's also about making the world a better place. BeyGOOD, her philanthropic initiative, has touched countless lives. In recognition of her humanitarian efforts, she received the 2020 BET Humanitarian Award—a testament to the powerful work she's done and continues to do.

"I am hugely proud of the work we have done over a decade at BeyGOOD, here in the US and around the world," Beyoncé says on the foundation's website. "From scholarships to the water crisis in Burundi, to helping families during Hurricane Harvey in my hometown, Houston, it has been beyond fulfilling to be of service."

The work that BeyGOOD has done—from supporting Black-owned small businesses during the COVID-19 pandemic to providing financial help to young women pursuing creative arts, music, theater, or African American studies—is simply a reflection of Beyoncé's charitable heart. She's a

role model for using influence to create positive change, reminding us that giving back is the true measure of success.

And let's talk about how Beyoncé leads by example. Her special guest appearance during Coldplay's 2016 Super Bowl halftime show wasn't just a performance; it was a powerful message. Beyoncé made sure the world was

paying attention, having dancers in *Black Panther*-inspired outfits while singing lyrics that called out **racial injustice**. Her commitment to movements like Black Lives Matter is more about action than words. She shows us that being a true leader means standing up for what's right, even when it's tough.

So, what's the secret behind Beyoncé's success as a business mogul? It's her ability to always think bigger, to push boundaries and set trends instead of following them. A prime example is the launch of her hair care brand, Cécred, in February 2024. Developed over six years, Cécred offers products designed for all hair types, reflecting Beyoncé's commitment to inclusivity and innovation. Beyond product development, she established an annual $500,000 grant in collaboration with her BeyGOOD foundation to support cosmetology students and professional hairstylists, demonstrating her dedication to empowering others in the beauty industry.

With Beyoncé at the helm, her business empire continues to thrive and shape the future. From revolutionizing fashion to championing social justice, she's showing us that true success is measured by the impact you make in the lives of others. And as she continues to expand her empire, one thing's clear: There are no limits when it comes to Beyoncé.

WORDS TO KNOW

philanthropy: donating money, goods, or time to help others, often through charitable organizations

fast fashion: trendy clothes manufactured quickly and cheaply, but often at a cost to the environment and the people who make them

athleisure: clothing designed for athletic activities that is also suitable for casual, everyday wear

racial injustice: unfair treatment or discrimination based on race

THE WORLD AT THE TIME

In 2023:

- The World Health Organization declared the end of the COVID-19 global health emergency.
- The Walt Disney Company celebrated its 100th anniversary, marking a century of beloved characters and magical stories.
- Music historians and cultural critics recognized "50 Years of Hip Hop," which culminated in a star-studded salute at the annual Grammy Awards.

WHAT DO YOU THINK?

- What do you think it takes to balance being a performer, a business owner, and a philanthropist like Beyoncé?
- If you could team up with Beyoncé to work on a project, what would you want to create together?

10

A Legacy That Inspires

*The best thing is looking back and
realizing how incredible life is.*
—BEYONCÉ KNOWLES

Beyoncé's story isn't just about talent—it's about how one woman can change the world. From her chart-topping hits to her fearless **activism** to being a fashionista, actress, filmmaker, and role model, Beyoncé has left a lasting mark on our hearts and minds.

Throughout her career, Beyoncé has shattered glass ceilings and redefined what it means to be a global celebrity. But guess what? Behind all the glitz and glamour, she's just as committed to her family. Balancing her superstar status with being a hands-on mom to Blue Ivy, Rumi, and Sir isn't easy, but she makes it look effortless. In a world where fame often comes at a personal cost, Beyoncé shows us that you can have it all . . . if you're willing to work for it.

At home, Beyoncé is more than a superstar. She's a mom, creating a world where her kids can thrive. Together with Jay-Z, they've built a space where creativity and confidence are everyday magic.

Being a mom has transformed Beyoncé in ways that go beyond the stage. She's said it herself: "I feel more beautiful than I've ever felt because I've given birth. I have never felt so connected, never felt like I had such a purpose on this earth." That purpose shines through in everything she does, from fighting for gender equality to pushing for social justice. She's doing it for her kids, and for kids everywhere.

And speaking of kids, Blue Ivy is already turning heads. Imagine being nine years old and winning a Grammy—right beside your mom! That's exactly what Blue Ivy did in 2021, becoming the second-youngest Grammy winner ever. She earned the award for Best Music Video for "Brown Skin Girl," where she contributed vocals and cowrote a verse, celebrating Black beauty and heritage alongside Beyoncé.

But let's not stop there. Beyoncé's influence stretches far beyond her family. She's inspired millions around the world, especially women and people of color, to stand tall and embrace their power. Whether it's through her music, her business ventures, or her philanthropy, Queen Bey is all about challenging the status quo and empowering others to do the same.

"I used to feel like the world wanted me to stay in my little box. And Black women often feel underestimated," Beyoncé said in *Homecoming*, a 2019 documentary film that she wrote and directed that told the story of her being the first Black woman to headline the Coachella Valley Music and Arts Festival. "I wanted us to be proud of not only the show but the process. Proud of the struggle." Thousands of fans called the event "Beychella" even before the critics praised her performance, which opened with "Crazy in Love" accompanied by a New Orleans–style marching band and included yet another Destiny's Child reunion with Kelly Rowland and Michelle Williams.

What else would we expect from someone who sold two-hundred-plus million records, earned thirty-plus Grammy Awards, and is the most successful Black touring artist in history? Small wonder that *Time* magazine included her as one of the one hundred women who have defined the twenty-first century so far.

As we wrap up this book on Beyoncé's incredible journey, one thing is beyond question: Her legacy is already massive, and she's still adding to it. But above all, Beyoncé is an inspiration—a living reminder that with talent, hard work, and a whole lot of heart, you can change the world.

So, what's next for Beyoncé? Well, in her own words, "The best is yet to come."

WORDS TO KNOW

activism: taking action to bring about change

THE WORLD AT THE TIME

In 2024:

- Apple launched its first AR (alternate reality) headset.
- Claudia Sheinbaum, an environmental scientist and former mayor of Mexico City, was elected to be Mexico's first female president.

WHAT DO YOU THINK?

- How do you think Blue Ivy feels about following in her mom's footsteps?
- What part of Beyoncé's journey do you find most inspiring?

Glossary

accolade: an award or special recognition for achievement

activism: taking action to bring about change

aesthetic: a particular style or approach to art and beauty

anthem: a song identified with a particular group or cause

apartheid: a system of racial segregation and discrimination

athleisure: clothing designed for athletic activities that is also suitable for casual, everyday wear

ballad: a slow, emotional song that tells a story

bona fide: genuine, authentic, or real

choreography: the art of creating and arranging dance movements

debut: the very first time someone or something is presented to the public

empowerment: confidence and control over your own life and decisions

fast fashion: trendy clothes manufactured quickly and cheaply, but often at a cost to the environment and the people who make them

genre: a category or type of art, music, or literature, characterized by its style, form, or content

geopolitical: relating to the influence of geography and politics on international relations

Givenchy: a famous French luxury fashion and perfume house

grossing: earning a certain amount of money before expenses are taken out

icon: a person or thing widely admired and recognized as a symbol of something

infamous: well-known for something bad or negative

infectious: easily spread from one person to another

innovative: introducing new ideas or methods; original and creative in thinking

introspective: looking inward to examine your own thoughts and feelings

Louvre: a world-renowned art museum located in Paris, France, and home to important works like the *Mona Lisa*

mesmerized: completely captivated or fascinated by something

minimalist: characterized by extreme simplicity of form or design

moderation: doing or having something in a balanced way

mogul: a powerful and influential person in business or industry

Motown: a legendary record label from Detroit that became the heart of soul and R&B music

persona: a social role or character adopted by an individual

philanthropy: donating money, goods, or time to help others, often through charitable organizations

racial injustice: unfair treatment or discrimination based on race

reconciliation: the act of restoring friendly relations

resilience: the ability to bounce back from tough times and keep going strong

resonated: created a feeling of shared experience or understanding

Southern Gothic: a literary genre characterized by its setting in the southern United States and its focus on themes of decay, the grotesque, and social issues

sportswashing: using sports to make people forget about bad actions or policies

symbolism: the use of objects or images to represent deeper ideas

testament: proof or evidence that something is true

versatility: the ability to adapt to different activities or roles

Warsan Shire: a Somali-British poet known for her powerful verses on themes of identity, displacement, and love

zydeco: a lively music and dance style from Louisiana that blends African American and Creole traditions with a touch of French flair

Timeline

- **1981**: Born September 4, in Houston, Texas

- **1990**: Forms the group Girl's Tyme

- **1996**: Girl's Tyme rebrands as Destiny's Child

- **1998**: Destiny's Child releases self-titled debut album

- **2003**: Releases debut solo album, *Dangerously in Love*

- **2006**: Stars in *Dreamgirls* and releases the album *B'Day*

- **2008**: Marries Jay-Z and releases the album *I Am . . . Sasha Fierce*

- **2012**: Gives birth to daughter Blue Ivy Carter

- **2013**: Headlines the Super Bowl XLVII

halftime show; surprise release of the visual album *Beyoncé*

2016: Releases the visual album *Lemonade*; performs as a special guest for Coldplay's Super Bowl 50 halftime show

2017: Gives birth to twins Rumi and Sir Carter

2020: Releases the musical album and film *Black Is King*; receives the Humanitarian Award at the BET Awards, honoring her BeyGOOD initiative; Blue Ivy Carter becomes the second-youngest Grammy winner

2022: Releases the album *Renaissance*

2024: Releases the album *Cowboy Carter*

2025: Wins Album of the Year at the Grammy Awards for *Cowboy Carter*

Selected Bibliography

Betancourt, Bianca. "The Beyoncé Album That Changed Everything." *Harper's Bazaar*. December 15, 2023.

Carlin, Shannon. "6 Revelations from Beyoncé's New Album *Renaissance*." *Time*. July 29, 2022.

Gonzalez, Erica. "Blue Ivy Carter Is Now a Grammy Winner." *Harper's Bazaar*. March 14, 2021.

Hautman, Nicholas. "*Destiny's Child: Where Are the 6 Members Now?*" *US Magazine*. February 8, 2021.

Jones, Okla. "The Legacy of Beyoncé." *Essence*. September 3, 2021.

Lavette, Lavaille, and Anastasia Magloire Williams. *Beyoncé: A Little Golden Biography*. Golden Books, 2023.

Moss, Caroline, and Sinem Erkas. *Work It, Girl: Beyoncé Knowles*. Frances Lincoln Children's Books, 2021.

Paul, Larisha. "How Beyoncé Has Used Her Concert Films to Tell Us Who She Really Is." *Rolling Stone*. November 27, 2023.

Tinsley, Omise'eke Natasha. *Beyoncé in Formation: Remixing Black Feminism*. University of Texas Press, 2018.

Vegara, Maria Isabel Sanchez, and Jade Orlando. *Little People, BIG DREAMS: Beyoncé*. Frances Lincoln Children's Books, 2024.

Warren, Sarah, and Geneva Bowers. *Beyoncé: Shine Your Light*. Clarion Books, 2019.

Wilkins, Ebony Joy. *Trailblazers: Beyoncé: Queen of the Spotlight*. Random House Books for Young Readers, 2020.

About Patricia Pete

Patricia Pete grew up in Sarasota, Florida, and earned a BFA in film from Ringling College of Art and Design. A lifelong storyteller, she finds inspiration in narratives of all kinds—whether on the page, the screen, or beyond. When she's not writing, she enjoys journaling, reading, and taking dramatic close-up photos of food.

About Ryan G. Van Cleave

Dr. Ryan G. Van Cleave is the author of dozens of fiction, nonfiction, and poetry books for both children and adults. When Ryan's not writing, he's crisscrossing the country, teaching writing at schools throughout the United States. He also moonlights as The Picture Book Doctor™, helping celebrities write stories for kids and bring them to life on the page, stage, and screen.

About Ariyana Taylor

Ariyana Taylor—also known as Fumisketchies—is a freelance illustrator and character designer based in Brooklyn, New York. In 2020, she graduated from the Fashion Institute of Technology with a bachelor's degree in illustration. Since then, she has illustrated for both small businesses and larger animation companies including Titmouse, Netflix, and Bent Image Lab.

Printed in the United States
by Baker & Taylor Publisher Services